SOUL
SENSE

YOUR BREAKTHROUGH TO
SOUL-FULL LIVING AND LEADERSHIP

T0163654

ADRIENNE ARLEN DUFFY

SOUL SENSE
YOUR BREAKTHROUGH TO SOUL-FULL LIVING AND LEADERSHIP

© 2017 Adrienne Arlen Duffy

Published in New York, New York, by Morgan James Publishing. Morgan James is a trademark of Morgan James, LLC. www.MorganJamesPublishing.com

The Morgan James Speakers Group can bring authors to your live event. For more information or to book an event visit The Morgan James Speakers Group at www. TheMorganJamesSpeakersGroup.com.

ISBN 9781683502784 paperback
ISBN 9781683502791 eBook
Library of Congress Control Number: 2017905331

Cover and Interior Design by:
Chris Treccani
3 Dog Design

In an effort to support local communities, raise awareness and funds, Morgan James Publishing donates a percentage of all book sales for the life of each book to Habitat for Humanity Peninsula and Greater Williamsburg.

Get involved today! Visit
www.MorganJamesBuilds.com

CONTENTS

FOREWORD

For thousands of years, people the world over have given a name to the vital force in life, which we know in English as *soul*. Over time soul has also taken on metaphorical significance as well, meaning *center, essence, and truth*. It is truly one of the most powerful terms in our language, as noble as is its opposite, *soulless*, is terrifying. From Plato, who referred to the soul as "the winged thing," to Ray Charles, who helped launch the soul music phenomenon by combining gospel music with rhythm and blues, what we see is that there is a numinous force that grounds and centers us. While soul is a vital image in theology, psychology (the very study of the soul), art, literature, and music, it has been overlooked as a critical aspect of leadership. To observe that an individual is soulful is to suggest that he or she is true, authentic, and centered; to say that an individual is soulless alludes to its opposite, which is spurious, inauthentic, and off-kilter.

For me, the importance of Adrienne Arlen Duffy's book, *Soul Sense*, lies in how it addresses one of the central issues of our time, which is the sense of meaninglessness and lack of balance claimed by so many modern people in the midst of more plenitude and technological advancement than the world has ever seen.

And yet in these pages, the reader will encounter one of the key (and perhaps only) solutions for such a situation. All that is needed is for the soul to be called home again, what the author refers to as a "soul call." For Adrienne, this means a series of practices and contemplations that can help the reader to find his or her bearings, which is to say their true orientation, their voice, their truth. This is the royal road back to meaning or purpose in our work and lives.

For many, this will be a radical way to look at living, leadership, and entrepreneurship. No worries. With a slight shift of perspective, the truth of the soul's own wisdom can be seen as welcome and rejuvenating. To honor the deepest soundings of one's true self, and by turn one's truest vocation, is to embark upon a new journey. *Soul Sense* provides the kind of guidance that has always been needed to shape effective and reliable leaders. Its most authentic advice is a reminder, in the author's words, that "this book is about choice and the belief that we do have the capacity, wisdom, and power to respond to whatever the universe tosses our way."

The book's central advice is elegantly simple: Use your freedom to choose to live with a sense of integrity and dignity, turn inward and focus, and proclaim a joyous "Yes!" And if you develop what Adrienne refers to as "Soul Sense," you will be rewarded with a consciously creative and soulful life.

Phil Cousineau

San Francisco

SOUL SENSE

Through the hundreds of people I have guided toward the realization of their full potential, and in the hundreds of workshops I have facilitated, one message has emerged universally over others:

"We want something in addition to the achievement of goals and results. We are people who aim high and take risks, but we also long to have meaning, live from the highest values and to be grounded. How can we create a more centered, purposeful life and workspace, in this era of constant change, chaos, and minute-by-minute progress?"

Soul Sense is the answer. The Soul Sense Process™ comprised of Soul Call, Soul Fire and Soul Care that is described in this book puts a name, conscious intent, and practice to Soul-Full living. Listening to your Soul Call, stoking your Soul Fire, and practicing Soul Care brings depth, growth and balance.

Soul Sense can be thought of as common sense seasoned with the sixth. It is what you know as *good*, and *right,* and *just* in your personal and professional lives, while embracing the powers of intuition that transcend such definitions. Soul Sense is logical and instinctual, practical and untamed.

Developing Soul Sense is a doorway to living your life with elevated consciousness and accountability.

Tuning into and trusting your Soul Sense brings increasing fulfillment to your life, and to the lives of those around you.

The courageous choice to honor your Soul Sense, ultimately, is up to you—and it is my joy and intention to lead you toward this profound gift.

Your Soul Sense awaits….

INTRODUCTION

THE GOLDEN OPPORTUNITY

Leaders and entrepreneurs, recent college graduates and midcareer executives, parents sitting around the dinner table with their children—everyone is feeling unprecedented pressure. While it's true that throughout history the North American economy and citizenry have faced their fair share of challenges, never before have outside conditions forced themselves upon us at such an accelerated pace. As technology ceaselessly impacts many aspects of our business and personal lives, disruption, volatility, and change are on the rise.

We have reached a tipping point, and with this increased external pressure comes a decreased internal sense of control and confidence. So, what is the opportunity? What is needed?

To counteract and counterbalance this trend of volatility, we need an expansion of consciousness: Each of us must sit, pause, and ask ourselves, "How can I become more aware and attentive as I go about my day? What can I do to better connect with all that is positive and grounding? How do I maintain my equilibrium moving forward?"

Technological growth influences our lives in many ways, but tends to fall short when it comes to engaging our *soul*.

In my business, I see hundreds of seasoned leaders, young professionals, college students, and spouses of colleagues asking themselves—*even amid success*, "Why, if I have jumped through all the right hoops and have executed all the proper strategies, do I sometimes feel so empty, unfulfilled, unbalanced, or unfocused?"

Each of us conducts this sort of internal self-assessment from time to time. It's human nature to seek answers—to ask ourselves powerful and soulful questions, such as "Where am I, after all this time and effort? Who am I? *Why* am I doing what I do?"

"You're not alone in this kind of wondering," I tell people. "Within these questions of *who am I* and *what's my purpose*—and the experiences that drive them—lie huge opportunities. Your choice is to search out the missing pieces and integrate them so that you are more whole and more grounded—and that's a positive."

Volatility on the outside is forcing people to look inward—and this can be a very good thing even under the most difficult circumstances. The younger generation, just out of college, is not exempt from sensing this lack of predictability—they too are aware that they need to learn how to better adapt and flow with it. This awareness, combined with the urge to remain curious and to learn, fortunately, resides in all of us. We just need a slight readjustment of our vision—a new point of view.

Extreme conditions are creating a catalyst for change, and that potential for change is exhilarating. Most people can taste it. People in all stages of their lives are telling me, "I want to reconnect with that freedom I first set out to achieve. I want to connect with that early sense of passion, awe, and vigor that fueled me. I want to figure out how to maintain my sense of direction and motivation no matter what happens around me."

The problem that so many people are facing right now is *the reckoning*—it is humbling to find yourself questioning where you stand, despite all your efforts, successes, and triumphs. The recognition that you are vulnerable can be disquieting. The understanding, too, that you are increasingly responsible for establishing and maintaining your own centering and nurturing your own soul can be a bit overwhelming.

But we all have the innate capacity to grow, and by developing your Soul Sense, you can start leading your own life in a more grounded and soulful way, and you can start to more effectively, successfully, and soulfully lead others.

So what does it mean to say "Yes!" to soulful living and soulful leadership? What does Soul mean in the context of these pages? How do we begin here to explore our Soul Sense?

The concept of Soul, of course, means something different to each of us, and throughout history many have endeavored to define it. For the purposes of this conversation, we'll look at Soul as the creative core and the *life-affirming presence of the spark, fire, and breath of full aliveness.* We'll look at soulful living as the cultivation of this core.

The challenge of living a more soulful and grounded life entails taking the first step—it entails some work. It entails holding certain conversations—soulful conversations—with yourself first, and then with those you care about and perhaps those you influence.

We are standing before the frontier of a new way of living, of leading, and of being led. We want meaningful work and meaningful lives and are seeking to be grounded from within—which might seem to be a paradox as the virtual world presses closer against the real one, but which is a golden opportunity to grow while owning our highest potential.

CHAPTER 1

CONNECTING THE DOTS, WEAVING THE THREADS

A very successful young entrepreneur of about forty approached me at a seminar recently, and blurted out, "Some unforeseen changes are affecting my business and the markets we serve, and it looks like I may not have a business by the end of this year!"

This man's absolute sense of disruption and loss of control was in part being driven by the rapid rise of technology and the impact of volatility on the business model that had for many decades been reliable and profitable. But because we have reached the tipping point, where change is constant and volatility and disruption are on the rise, many people are becoming ungrounded.

Through our discussion, he was wisely able to discern that he needed to keep his center, exercise, focus on his values, and focus on loving his family.

This is one man's story, but you don't have to look far to see that a large number of people are losing control over what they thought was predictable. Some are fighting desperately to maintain the world they once knew, but it is gone; others are seizing the opportunity to change their point of view and grow.

This forty-year-old entrepreneur became conscious of the soulful choice he could make in regard to handling his struggle—there was an opportunity. And by fundamentally recognizing the need to stay grounded, he was heading in the right direction.

"You'll get through this volatile time with grace," I told him. "You *are* getting through it."

This man did more than just overcome the challenges that faced him; he is now living an even more fulfilling and successful life than he was before. Wouldn't it be great if people at similar points in their lives or careers could do what this man did—*on a conscious level, develop their Soul Sense, starting today*?

Times are challenging sounds so cliché, but times *are* challenging. *You have a choice* is also cliché, but you *do* have a choice—and now, more than ever, is the time to consciously take advantage of it.

A HOST OF CHOICES

When the bottom of what they once thought they could count on falls out, some people choose to be victims. They make everybody else guilty-as-charged and complain about all the wrong being done to them. In doing so, they give away their power and the opportunity to live more soulfully.

Others attempt to control more of the uncontrollable factors we all invariably face. These are the people you see pedaling faster and faster just to maintain the illusion they've got everything covered. The energy they expend is astounding, difficult to sustain, and eventually depleting.

And still others attempt to stick to the familiar tactics and strategies that worked in the past, not wanting to acknowledge that the present is urging them to do something unfamiliar—which entails risk.

Even for those with the entrepreneurial spirit, which is generally regarded as "risk-friendly" as opposed to "risk-averse," a new type of risk can bring on fear or doubt. It is natural every once in a while to find ourselves stuck, no matter what our level of experience or success is. And those ruts we get stuck in might seem to come about more frequently today, because of the rapid pace by which everything is moving.

But you have this book in your hands because you are ready to break away from the roads most frequently traveled.

This book can be a doorway to your new journey, and I'm glad you've opened it!

Perhaps you are ready to respond differently now to the circumstances that are presenting themselves. You are an open mind and courageous spirit. You've experienced success on a variety of levels, but you know that there is more beneath the surface.

Right now, you can make a choice to develop Soul Sense, to step back from the old landscape and step up to that great telescope into the soul. Think of those machines you plunk a few coins in so that you can gaze across an entire city skyline—everything gleams gold. When you take this kind of deep, broad, long survey, you understand that you carry some of that gold within. When you put your eye right up to that small circle and change your point of view, you begin to see that amid disruption, you can make the choice *right now* to pay more attention to your soul. Stick with that deeper level of soul attention, and you can alter the way change has been controlling you.

Start by telling yourself this: "I am going to receive what's happening right now as an opportunity to evolve. I'm going to grow and expand not only my own potential, but also my leadership or way of being in the world. I am going to be fully accountable and continue to believe in and live into an abundant future."

Balance and unite the distant gleaming landscape with a focus on your inner golden values, as our entrepreneur did when his professional life began to fall apart. Once you start doing all the things you already do through the golden lens of Soul, you reestablish a sense of integrity and dignity in terms of responding to what you can't control. That is, you become more grounded.

You begin to build an expanded platform to stand upon, one that is more fortified than the one you have been standing on until now. This platform rests upon all of your past successes, but enables the more soulful future you are ready to live into now.

Let me reiterate this point: Nobody is asking you to completely turn from the wonderful life you have built thus far. You can build upon your triumphs of the past, and surpass them in ways you may not have yet dreamed of, with an *intentional* focus on soulful living.

This book is the opening of a conversation and an invitation to develop your Soul Sense. It is an exploration of inspiration and potential.

SOUL IS STORY:
THE CHARACTER IS YOU

Soulful living and leadership does not require learning a new terminology—*vision, purpose, strategy, value creation, outcomes,* and so on—all the well-known concepts still have meaning. You will just mine deeper into them so that moving forward you can more consciously bring Soul to all the chapters of your life story.

People take many routes to attain soulful living and leadership. Sometimes all we need is a nudge; other times it takes a significant upheaval and a permanent departure from the world as we once knew it. The young entrepreneur who knew he would soon have to start from scratch came to his crossroad—his reckoning—and made a choice to stay true to himself and evolve. Many of the most famous entrepreneurs in the world have done this multiple times.

Most of us are familiar with Steve Jobs's life story: He told part of it in the commencement speech he gave to the 2005 graduating class at Stanford University. The speech touches upon the value of staying your course, of taking risks, of dusting yourself off when your heart and livelihood are suddenly tossed out the window, and of chasing wholeheartedly what you are most curious about.

Jobs—who had been diagnosed in 2004 with pancreatic cancer—spoke to his audience about how to live before dying. He said you have to *trust in something*. He said it was "impossible to connect the dots looking forward" but easier to connect them "looking backwards ten years later." He was a man who understood human potential, work, love, and soul, and how if you connected these things—you could ignite the world. He had Soul Sense.

We all have a story. When we try to make sense of this story—or when we try to connect the dots—we often turn inward. We naturally begin to soul search—it is an ancient, perennial, and powerful process.

When I connect the dots of my life, the reason I do the work I do today rings clear as a bell. My story reflects an experience that is common to many: At some point in our lives, we have all "rubbed up" against conflicting community ideologies, social structures, and family dynamics that catalyze our growth.

I grew up the child of an upper-middle-class family, with a Jewish father and a non-Jewish mother. Our house, in the suburbs of Chicago, was set smack dab in the middle of the Jewish side and the Catholic side of the neighborhood. If I were writing a memoir, nobody would believe me, but it's true: We lived right between dozens of Jewish families and dozens of Catholic families, and we attended a Methodist church.

In my neighborhood, the Jewish kids went to the public school. The few Protestant kids, like me, went there also. The Catholics, of course, went to Catholic school. The path to both schools ran right up the center between the two main streets. I recall instances when the Catholic kids would ride their bikes by and try to splash me with mud because they thought I was Jewish, and then at school not being part of the in-group, because I was not.

At age six or seven, I was at school daily, feeling like an outcast.

Of course, I had friends, but when some of my Jewish friends had me over, their grandparents refused to acknowledge my presence. Granted, some of them were Holocaust survivors or had relatives who were, but I didn't understand this as a young girl. All I really understood was that I was different.

I was also overweight. And yes, I was also teased and tormented about that constantly.

I grew up in a wonderful family, but there was a sub-dynamic at play in our community. I used to wonder what it all meant. And then, right before I went into junior high—I found music.

Playing the flute requires a lot of breathwork; it is centering. Playing the flute was where I could explore and find my potential; it was an experience completely separate from the odd dynamic going on around me. Music was a special place where I could shine; it supplied a soulful shoulder I could lean on and a community I could unite with outside of the turbulence I was experiencing.

Aristotle walked the Garden of Muses for good reason—he went there for inspiration, and most of us will instinctively find a way to whatever it is that nourishes our Soul most, when our Soul most needs it. But can we stay the soulful course? How can we? Is now the time to walk with our muse?

The times I grew up in were turbulent, as they are today. The structures that were in place that were supposed to give people an identity stirred up more questions for me than answers. By age ten, I'd been witness to religious, racial, and physical discrimination. I was in the middle of the perfect storm from which to kick off a journey of personal growth and transformation—it was the turbulence itself that spurred me to creatively seek out some rhythm, some order and perspective.

Confusion led me to opportunity: Life was an adventure, full of obstacles, to be sure; but, with music, life was also full of beauty. Music was a path I could authentically follow, and I now understand it represented—on the outside—the inside rhythm of my soul. The choice to view this adversity as an opportunity provided the early seeds of developing my Soul Sense.

As a child forced to walk many lines, I instinctively understood the importance of balancing the outer and inner worlds, and the power of following your bliss.

Many people tell me that this "child's knowing" is what they are seeking again now—many of us knew in our youth exactly where our soul's rhythm could be found. Our muses were always close by, but then the business of life set in—we started making a living, parenting, and "being busy." We lost touch consciously with what moved our Soul.

The good news is: All we need to do is shift our point of view and re-align ourselves with what we once knew and have never forgotten.

It might help too to keep in mind what Steve Jobs said to those Stanford grads: "Don't let the noise of others' opinions drown out your inner voice, heart, and intuition."

These are words we all need to hear from time to time. But again, to keep your inner voice, heart, and intuition afloat amid storms, you have to take the time to locate, listen to, and know them first.

REFLECT, RECKON, RISK, THEN FLOW

Long ago, I set my heart on music. Eventually too one day I set my mind on losing the weight I had carried my entire life. I chose to live life as "mobile" as opposed to fixed; that is, I chose to live my life according to something that music embodies: flow and inspiration.

I chose too to travel, finally venturing to Greece recently—where inspiration dwells, where some of history's greatest philosophers held daily conversations centered on Soul, and where some of the world's most influential modern mentors continue to find the inspiration to coach and motivate others.

Walking in Greece, I reflected back on my own path as a coach, and how I moved from learning and creating my own music as a girl to creating my own music business as a young woman—where I taught music to dozens of young talented people. This work was inspiring, soulful work, but even moving in that direction, I hit a place of reckoning.

The turning point occurred when I realized part of the block I was facing with one of my most challenging and challenged students—who had huge potential—was because of her home life. It then struck me that I could probably do more to help young people by working with their parents.

I did not shift my music business to include adults—I shifted my business, and my life, entirely. I turned to working with professional-level adults—believing inspiration would then blossom and flow not just through their work lives, but also through their home lives. This new Soul expression was equally as nourishing and impactful as the work I had done through music—it sparked the fire in me and inspired the people I worked with, just as music had.

Life presents us with multiple forms of Soul expression, and it's up to us to accept different invitations at different junctures of our lives.

I have a story. Jobs had a story. You have one, too. When I connect the dots of my stories, I understand why I am being called in these tumultuous times to talk about leadership and living from a soulful perspective. I have guided people using strategy for decades, and strategy works—but now amid the polarities of turmoil and abundant possibilities, I see that strategy alone is not enough.

Many people feel lost right now because their success seems somehow incomplete, or different than they expected. While their success is evident from the outside, they may somehow still feel empty about it on the inside. The Soul has a hunger—it wants to contribute to the Soul of the world, and unless you are living and leading consciously, that hunger gnaws at you—it leaves you wanting more. Eventually, it forces you to ask questions.

It's not unusual in tumultuous times to catch a glimpse of ourselves in the mirror and ask our reflection, "Who am I? How did I get here? Does what I'm doing matter?"

Nor is it unusual to purposefully carve time out to assess the life we are leading. Either way, reflection is essential; reflection can lead to the reckoning that spurs our expansion. In order to get to the point of reckoning and discover your "soul spark," you have to embrace mystery and risk.

On the other side of risk—when you break through—you'll gain back those first glimpses of truth you understood when you were young and believed everything was possible. You already possess the power of hindsight: All the walls that have been placed before you at different phases of your life looked ten feet thick when you faced them, right? But now—don't many of them appear as thin as paper?

When you choose to accept that risk is an inherent and unavoidable part of life, you will re-enter the natural cyclic flow of life. You'll see walls as opportunities to break through and to grow. You'll be able to release your grip on everything you cannot control and open up the space and energy to more consciously experience Soul Sense. The Soul Sense Process™ enables you to hear your Soul Call, stoke your Soul Fire, and spin and weave gold by applying the Golden Threads of Soul Care. In doing so, you will generate more inner vitality for yourself and more value for the world.

CHAPTER 2

SOUL CALL, SOUL FIRE, SOUL CARE: AN OVERVIEW

Author Mona Simpson, in the eulogy she wrote for her brother, Steve Jobs, shared with the world his final words: "Wow, wow, wow."

Whether you are a religious person or not; whether you are a mystical person or not—it is hard not to be stunned by both the simplicity and the power of such a statement. We cannot know if Jobs said this in response to something he was seeing in the beyond— perhaps "the light"? We cannot know what physical sensations were coursing through his body in his final moments. We cannot equate those words to his gratefulness to be surrounded by those he loved most, or to fear, or to the simple recognition he would not have another day to *be*.

Who among us wouldn't want to feel more "wow" in our everyday lives? We can take a big step in that direction by choosing to live more consciously from a Soul-full place.

But how?

Carl Jung once said that once the disease is named the healing can begin. I believe there is great power in naming our desires, especially in naming the desire one is trying to fulfill when venturing toward a new journey or pilgrimage. When we begin taking more conscious steps toward Soul, we can begin to hear its call—and in time, fire will follow.

To create a simplified context for this conscious development of Soul Sense in everyday life, we use the triad of Soul Call, Soul Fire, and Soul Care.

THE SOUL SENSE PROCESS™

SOUL CALL:
THE GOLDEN DOOR

In life, there are essentially two types of calls that correspond to two types of growth. The first call, related to "outer" growth, comes to us from adventure, travel, success, material goods, and pleasure. The second call, related to "inner" growth, encourages us to reflect, deepen, explore, and discover.

Soul Call is:
- an inner call to name a truthful life intention
- the desire to be true to owning and cultivating your fullest potential
- the creation of value in the world by transforming that desire or intention into a form that will make a meaningful contribution outside of yourself

By acting upon Soul's call, we can experience both outer growth and inner growth, and when we consciously wed our outer growth to our inner growth, we can take quantum leaps in our lives. This is living from the Soul's Call.

Living this way, we can transform our selves and our lives as we never have before. We can integrate a desire to succeed with a desire to soulfully and creatively contribute. Creativity is available to all of us—to see and to use in our everyday work and our everyday life.

Yes, with our successes of the past, many of us have been very effective at responding to the opportunity, risk, reward, and potential of our outer growth. But what we can now choose to do is expand our view of success to include an inner, paralleling call—a Soul Call.

Unifying Soul with *success as we have known it*, we take that outer and inner gold we hold, and work it as the alchemist does—we expand creatively so that all we do becomes a reflection of our highest potential and best self. Life reflects our gold!

Soulfulness is about expanding and being in touch with your deepest reason for *why* you are doing what you do. It entails literally breathing "new" life into our present one. What my breathwork was long ago to my flute playing and music, Soul is to success.

Wow is a small word with great power, but living with Soul Call more consciously doesn't require that all of our contributions be life-altering and enormous. If you show up with your best self daily, judgment falls away concerning the magnitude of your contribution, and every opportunity becomes a chance to live more soulfully.

That's right: Paying attention to your Soul Call acknowledges your potential, fortifies your purpose by delving into *why*, and reduces judgment. It leads to a greater fueling of your Soul Fire.

SOUL FIRE:
TOUCHING THE GOLD

Most great leaders or amazing people you have known are stoking their Soul Fire. These people light up the room.

Soul Fire is:
- energeia, which is a renewing and vital form of life force energy that integrates mind, body, and soul
- the fuel that inspires and incites actions in pursuit of the Soul Call
- the extraordinary experience of Soul-full living

People who are just going through the motions and measuring their success by "outer growth" only have not *lost* their Soul Fire, they have just *lost touch* with it.

Steve Jobs may have had infamous moments of being a challenging person to work for, but he was clearly in touch with his creativity and his Soul Fire. He was also committed to inner growth. His ability to create and to inspire creativity was universal, active, and timeless. His Soul Fire was unmistakably powerful, renewing, and far-reaching—it was not extinguished until *after* his final "wow."

The beauty of Jobs's departing *wows* is that each of us can imagine in our own minds what the *wows* contained, so we can relate. The beauty too is that we can be confident that the *wows* contained everything—for in beauty often lies the simplest of missing pieces either you, or others around the world, are looking for. Beauty beckons us to our inner creative core, and inspires us to connect. Just listen to your favorite song and you are transformed—a fire is lit within you.

Imagine how your universe would shift if you listened to your Soul Call, decided to consciously step forward into that state of risk and mystery, and lit your Soul Fire. Might you not start to travel through each day as if your favorite song were playing—as if it were written for you? Wouldn't there be an extra vitality in your step—at work, at home, with friends and family? Wouldn't you walk into a room and inspire a few additional *wows*?

SOUL CARE:
THE GOLDEN THREADS

On his way out of this world, Jobs connected to it all by remaining amazed. In his last breath, he actually utilized one of the tools of what I call Soul Care, and breathed the breath of life. Say the word "wow" out loud right now and you'll know what I mean.

Soul Care is the conscious and intentional practice that supports soulful living. Soul Care practices can be:

- Grounding—they support the balance of the body and mind with the soul's inner rhythm. They support the inner growth journey.
- Nurturing—they assist in consciously creating and cultivating a healthy environment for both inner and outer growth.

- Healing—when excessive demands or stress
  are causing harm or stagnation, they can be
  transformative or rebalancing.

To sustain a profoundly soulful and rewarding life
requires effort and constant renewal—it requires Soul
Care. Soul Care—though Jobs didn't call it that—is
essentially what he hoped Stanford's graduating class
of 2005 would practice.

Steve Jobs probably had no idea how many
millions more people would watch and share his
Stanford speech, but certainly he seemed to know that
universally people seek guidance on how to "get what
it means to be alive" before dying.

There is no denying that consciousness is rising.

People are developing Soul Sense by paying
attention to their Soul Call and fueling their Soul
Fire. They are sustaining and cultivating their Soul
Fire with Soul Care—that is, they are reacquiring
some of the most ancient tools we have in order to stay
centered amid the chaos.

People are finding ways to care for the soul by
creating safe, sound, trustful spaces and ways of
being for soulfulness to abound and expand—
weaving it all together with what I call the Golden

Threads, which are not only beautiful, but also pliable and durable.

CHAPTER 3

SOUL CALL:

QUESTIONING RESPONDING, AND LISTENING DEEPER STILL

Honoring your Soul Call allows you to bring creative intention to all you do. Your Soul Call is the gift that—when you decide to claim it—allows you to bring *your gift* into the world.

What is your gift? What is that urgency? Why is it more important than ever that you learn how to listen to your Soul Call?

When you listen to your Soul Call, you understand the urging potential—*your urging potential*—that demands you get to the heart of why in this very moment you sense there is more to your story.

To bounce back and learn from insult and injury—whether you are a young overweight girl living in the suburbs of Chicago as an outcast or a technology expert in Silicon Valley very publically losing your job—is a gift.

The gift may be disguised as an outer wound, but it is a wound that can bring about the power to question—it *calls* you to attention. It can spur you to rediscover and name your center—and this is where your creative freedom exists.

Soul Call is:
- an inner call to name a truthful life intention
- the desire to be true to owning and cultivating your fullest potential
- the creation of value in the world by transforming that desire or intention into a form that will make a meaningful contribution outside of yourself

---

THE SPARK

Earlier, I touched on two types of calls and two types of growth: inner and outer. Notice I didn't say inner "versus" outer. You don't have to choose to listen to one kind of call *or* the other; you can strive toward greater inner *and* outer growth simultaneously with greater alignment and integration. Responding knowingly, and equally, to the two calls strengthens us rather than depletes us. It grounds us, widens our stance, and furthers our reach. Beneath the surface our roots grow, and above ground our branches spread.

The beauty of making the extra effort to listen and respond to your inner call is that then all you do in response to your outer call becomes emboldened. There is no need to sacrifice money or some of the more outward symbols of success on your journey toward more soulful living, because as far as Soul is concerned, everything is unified.

When life has sent you the "I've had enough" message one too many times, it is time to face the reckoning. Stop, take a breath, and remind yourself what my father told me decades ago and that I have sung to myself many times since as a mantra: "You cannot look to outside structures for security. You are your own security. Look inward first."

Music took me inward—it was my creative center and still is one of them. Whenever I sense I'm drifting, I can return to music. You may find your center in any number of forms—inside and outside of your work. The point is to find it. Once you do, you will be able to center yourself on a regular basis—from work to play. Soul does not just find you while you are on vacation.

Listening for your Soul Call puts a purpose and context to all of your experience and actions. This can be as simple as consciously showing up every day with an awareness to help and serve others, or as bold as creating a new technology that will detect cancer at an early stage. Only your Soul knows for sure.

HEARING YOUR SOUL CALL

As you develop a more conscious awareness of Soul Sense at work—no matter how far along you are in this process—remember that all Soul asks of you is an invitation. Your Soul needs space, symbols, and conscious intent to thrive!

Soul does not just call out once so that we "do its bidding" and then are finished. Soul is ever-evolving and ever-expanding—once you turn toward it, you are never finished. Thankfully, Soul is also ever-forgiving. It is patient. It is always there.

Before reviewing the methods I turn to most frequently when coaching people on soulful living and leadership, I often mention Steve Winwood's song "Back in the High Life Again." For me, it reflects a core truth about Soul Call—especially the line: "All the doors I closed one time will open up again."

Initially, many people may find it difficult to discuss—let alone clarify—their Soul Call. Alternately, some people will be tempted to stop the soulful journey before they really even get started, fearing that once they acknowledge their Soul Call and get their Soul Fire burning again, it will require constant work or too much change—and if they lose it, all that work will be for nothing.

Winwood's lyrics about the doors reopening provide hope, I think—and a dose of reality—in regard to Soul Call: It isn't realistic for us to expect we'll live in a constant heightened state of Soul Call and Soul Fire. Even people who are totally committed to living soulfully have ever-evolving cycles—sometimes they need rest; sometimes they are challenged by the next threshold.

When I hear Winwood sing this song, I'm reminded that no matter where I am in my Soul work, I can still keep moving, I am not finished, there is more to be done. Each of us has our own Soul's touchstone song, and when we hear it, we are instantly energized and capable of reimagining. The key is to hold on to these Soul Calls or Moments of Soul, and make something out of them. But what do we do when, for example, nobody seems to be playing our touchstone Soul song? How can we more consciously and deliberately work to hear our Soul Call?

Working in leadership coaching over the past decades, I have seen that the Soul's Call can commonly appear in two ways: Soul Sounding and Moments of Soul. There may, of course, be as many ways a Soul calls as there are stars in the sky; however, these two ways can offer a beginning.

Soul Sounding often occurs when we are very young—often before the age of ten. Just as ultrasound seeks and reveals images of new life in the womb, Soul Sounding seeks the image of life potential within our psyche. Soul Sounding is a very intimate powerful urging that takes place when our conscious mind opens up to what our full potential could be; it is a *first impression* of how wonderful life could be if we were to express our full potential out in the world on a regular basis.

During my coaching sessions, I trigger a distant memory of Soul Sounding by posing the following multifaceted question: "What experience(s) did you have when you were young that offered you an image of what your life's potential could be? When did you first understand what your potential could be? When did you first get a sense of what ultimate fulfillment in life felt like?"

I can recollect two Soul Soundings in my life; the first, music, I've already shared with you. Very early on, I had a deep desire to express and create beauty in the world through music. The other was my desire at a young age to be a nurse—I wanted to help others heal. Although I never became a nurse, my career has put me in many situations where I can help others grow into their potential through the healing that occurs when they release the beliefs and habits that hold them back.

The Soul Sounding exercise can elicit answers rapidly, or not. Again, Soul needs an invitation— and conscious intent. Since the Soul can be very shy compared to our everyday ego, it might take some time for it to respond. Being relaxed and quiet, or even relearning how to experience being relaxed and quiet, might be the first step toward remembering and reclaiming one's formative Soul Sounding experiences.

Soul Sounding insights may come through all forms of active visualization or dreaming. I also suggest journaling, playing or listening to music, walking in nature, or deep listening through meditation. Whatever the method, I have discovered through my coaching that the wisdom of the Soul will not ignore a genuinely inspired and honest question: We get our answers and insights eventually. When the insights do come, this Soul Sounding exercise becomes a soulful "dot" to connect with later.

The second way I walk people through Soul Call is by asking them to begin to define and be consciously aware of what I call their "Moments of Soul." Moments of Soul can occur in everyday life, or when we are consciously in soul-seeking mode. In these Moments, life opens up our conscious mind to the remembrance of what brings us joy. Because joy ultimately is housed in our creative center, these moments serve as a way to reclaim our most authentic desires, where our most genuine dreams and longings for truth reside.

Moments of Soul usually have an extraordinary feeling of possibility attached to them—think "Wow, wow, wow!" They fill our psyches with a sense of regeneration and vitality that is the polar opposite of feeling numbed out. In college, while formally studying music, I had a Moment of Soul one day crossing campus when I felt the absolute joy and privilege to bring music to the world—everything felt connected and I will never forget the feeling of aliveness I felt on that day.

Moments of Soul connect us to our own Soul, but also to the whole we are a part of. These varied and intimate insights often serve to remind us that when we engage with the world through the lens of Soul, we contribute to creating value, which ultimately has life-affirming impact upon others. This life-affirming impact on others is what provides many of my Moments of Soul today.

As with the Soul Sounding exercise, reviewing your life for Moments of Soul requires a conscious effort. Journaling or completing a personal review to track and reflect on when these moments have appeared might take some quiet time and reflective space. You might start by asking: "What have I always loved to do that, while doing it, I feel vitalized and free? Throughout my life, what has made me feel most grateful? What am I doing when I feel most alive, present, creative, and generous?"

These insights too, will add to your Soul "dots" map. When several Soul dots become apparent, you can connect them and start to see a pattern. Once you see a pattern, you can name it, and then the Soul Call can begin to re-enter your imagination, pointing you in the direction of your fullest potential. The reimagining and naming that takes place during these Soul Sounding and Moments of Soul exercises can begin to open the interior doors you may have thought were sealed shut long ago; or they may allow you to see the power in what you are doing right now.

WHEN SOUL'S QUESTIONS
ARE ENTERTAINED, MEANING ENTERS

The journey of developing Soul Sense is one of the biggest opportunities you will ever have. When faced with an opportunity of this magnitude, you may experience resistance.

Asking the question, "What is the *highest reason* for learning the lessons I am faced with right now?" is critical to pushing past resistance in answering your Soul Call. Figuring out the answer to this question can help you transform this learning, and in turn help you on your journey to contribute to the world in a more meaningful way.

Don't just get to the Golden Door; walk through it. You are being called to learn, and in learning, you transform toward your fullest potential. You are being called to add deeper value with your gifts and abilities. Perhaps an age-old soulful question that comes from the Irish tradition might be helpful: "Are you getting what you came for?"

TURNING TOWARD THE LIGHT THAT IS SOUL FIRE

I understand that, as you more fully embrace your Soul Call and move closer to breaking through from one form of living to another, things might become uncomfortable, but trust that you don't have to drop everything at the Golden Door. You can carry forth the beliefs, habits, and strategies that truly work for you; just be sure that as you move forward, you bring Soul Sense consciously and rigorously to everything you still intend to use.

Yes, your ego will feel discomfort as you stand on the edge of the frontier of your Soul-full living and leadership—your ego will kick up a dust storm because ego alone cannot handle volatility and change. But your Soul will support you, and if you manage to merge your Soul to your ego, you can survive anything, and maybe even change your corner of the world in the process.

Imagine fields full of tall sunflowers—they are sturdy and bright, and when you look at them, you can hardly think about work or the daily challenges of life. These flowers have a golden Soul, just as much as you do. Take your Soul Call seriously, and your Soul will do exactly what those sunflowers do—it will turn to the light—to the fire—to the Soul Fire.

Continue to ask your *why* questions and to thrive on the notion of expansion, and your Soul will prove its vitality.

CHAPTER 4

SOUL FIRE:
IGNITING YOUR GIFTS

Soul Fire at work is visible—it calls your attention.

I was in my early twenties when I first witnessed Soul Fire moving through someone. Sitting in an audience of about one hundred people to watch flutist and teacher Marcel Moyse give a master class, I was in awe. Yes, the students who were performing for him were amazingly talented, but what struck me most was the way Moyse's entire being would light up, then rest, light up, then rest as each student approached him, played a solo, and awaited his feedback.

Moyse, who was sitting in a chair on stage, was approaching ninety, and not in excellent physical health. While his students played for him, he sat still, carefully listening. But as soon as he was ready to teach—to talk to them about their music—his posture and his face changed. He became animated by Soul Fire, energeia, the life force.

Considered the father of modern flute, Moyse taught many of today's greatest flutists, including James Galway. People who worked with Moyse refer to him as a vital and inspirational force. It's not surprising that his former student and world-class flutist Paula Robison said he had "incandescent eyes."

Moyse was a master of music, teaching, and breathwork. He inspired thousands of students to play music, but to also ask questions about gifts. Like anyone who infuses all they do with Soul Fire, his legacy lives on. The impact of his Soul Fire never truly extinguishes.

Trust in your questions. Trust in your passion. Trust in your fire.

Soul Fire is:
- energeia, which is a renewing and vital form of life force energy that integrates mind, body, and soul
- the fuel that inspires and incites actions in pursuit of the Soul Call
- the extraordinary experience of Soul-Full living in life

FROM THE WELLSPRING
OF VITALITY

The definition of the word "energeia" has evolved since the time and the way Aristotle used it: Latin for *work*, it is also the origin of the modern-day word "energy." A philosophical analysis of energeia and its relationship to *actuality* and *entelechy* is beyond the scope or purpose of this book, but in a nutshell, energeia and its various components—with their own multiple meanings—can be thought of as a combination of the following: energy, pleasure, happiness, perfection, movement, being at work, and being genuine. For our purposes, we'll think of it as *core* energy.

When you find your "music," or whatever activities connect you consciously to your Soul, your energeia is restored—life integrates. That is, you eventually stop separating work from home, or professional from personal. You bring the same conscious awareness to the board meeting as you do to an evening out with your family.

Energeia brings about the music of work and the work of your music, so into the flames we go!

Soul Fire, just like Earth, is multilayered: As you go deeper toward the center, fire turns from yellow, to orange, to blue. Those who live closest to this deepest hottest core of Soul Fire, the blue flame, tend to age more gracefully, have more vitality, and appear younger—they glow from the inside out! Marcel Moyse, despite his years, sat on that stage and transformed in front of me. Yes, he had to allow his *energeia* a few moments of rest, and would settle back into his chair between teaching moments, but he epitomized *life force*.

Those who are in touch with their *energeia* are unmistakably present. You can see them—and feel them—from a mile away. They are not only "professionally present," but emotionally present as well.

They may not have necessarily moved mountains all morning, but they practice alchemy daily—that is, they unite that universal gold we spoke of earlier with the gold they carry within. In showing up with their best selves daily, they make a daily, incremental, and powerful impact. At times, their main impact may be the simple act of sharing their gold to light up or inspire someone else who is in danger of drifting or "numbing out."

Who wouldn't be inspired to buff up their gold when someone is standing before them honoring their own?

People in touch with their Soul Fire encompass you—you can approach them—they are accessible. These people never seem able to retire in the official sense of the word, because they have shifted into a level of conscientious connecting, expanding, and contributing that is everlasting. They burn Soul energy as long as their health allows it, and even after they pass, their legacy lives on—still encompassing the world.

The energeia of Soul Fire changes your metabolism, your desire, and your brilliance. The great news is: Accessing energeia requires no outside stimulation or stimulants—you cannot go out and buy it—it is your most authentic and pure vital renewable source. You must tend to it, though, just as you must tend to your Soul Call, by going within.

BLAZING NEW TRAILS

Anchor yourself in the "why" questions and trust that they will always lead you to the wellspring of your Soul Fire. Think of "why" and all the answers it leads you to as combustible energy that gives you the inspiration and courage you need to make changes.

"Why" will also help you figure out *what* needs changing—is it your mindset, your activities, or outer structures?

Trust that these changes won't necessarily need to be extensive; rather, moving onward you will experience progress as an incremental expansion. Your Soul Call and your Soul Fire will be aligned—for fire always draws things to it—and with both in gear, you'll find yourself saying on a more regular basis,

"This is the life I'm living, and it couldn't be any better. Wow. I am on my path."

Once you engage the dual engines of Soul Call and Soul Fire, you consciously experience more frequent Moments of Soul on a daily basis. You see the Marcel Moyses of the world lighting up before your very eyes, and you become one of those people too.

You notice that when Soul Call and Soul Fire are aligned, they create space *and* a magnetizing force. They make room for and attract everything you need in the moment. Synchronicities increase; there are no coincidences. The people and situations you need appear before you, doors reopen.

You may have closed a few doors long ago, but remember, as Steve Winwood sings, you can reopen them at any time. Some fear may be attached: At times, it might seem simpler just to go on "dreaming" in the territory of Soul Call. Holding those Soul Call conversations with yourself and listening carefully, as we've discussed, does take energy, but Soul Fire really calls on us *to act on* what we have heard.

So, like the great goddess Nike, tether your wings—make them wings of fire—and get moving.

Soul Fire is there to fuel your actions and to help you take on challenges.

It might, in certain moments, feel easier to stop just short of taking on full responsibility for your energeia. You might fall back on the old standby, "Hey, I've done really well for myself. I'm successful. I'm all right!" You might mull over just how tightly shut those doors to your Soul could be and question if it's worth it. But remember, Soul Call and Soul Fire need one another—and feed one another. They work in unity—it's worth it!

No matter what phase of life you are in—young or old—you are capable of taking action. My mother, a talented painter who gave up her art to raise a family, returned to it in her late eighties after my father passed away. The first painting she made was for me—it was a bald eagle in flight.

With conscious awareness, you can make your own fire-fueled flight back and forth between your inner purpose and your outer goals, multiple times. The great news is that you'll evolve with each round-trip, and when Soul pops in and asks, "About your life, I'm curious—did you get what you came for?" you'll be able to answer with a resounding, "Yes!"

EXTRAORDINARY IN THE ORDINARY

You cannot connect the dots ahead of time, but you can remain transformed, vital, and soulful until your very last "wow." Furthermore, you can instill that Soul Fired "wow" with a sense that you have lived an extraordinary life.

Soul is pure, authentic, and present in that way. When you are paying attention to it and caring for it, it even allows challenges to be an important dot on the journey.

Remember, Soul trusts instinctively, and when you offer that trust back, you expand in ways that get you through volatile times with grace.

That's how our young entrepreneur in the first chapter handled his turbulent time—instinctively, he turned inward and focused where he needed to focus. Soul Sense got him through. Soul recognizes that it is one with that universal gold I've mentioned, and because that gold cannot possibly disappear all at once—or ever—*everything will be okay.*

Almost no one on the face of the planet gets a smooth, flat path laid out before them. In its ancient knowingness, Soul gives us opportunities, understanding that all our experiences—joyous and challenging—are enabling us to expand and are strengthening our contribution. Because Soul connects us to the whole we are a part of, it puts us in touch with our compassion as well. Those who live soulfully tend to be able to take both broad and varied points of view, which is part of the reason they succeed in almost anything they set out to do—even when they "fail," which is probably a word Soul doesn't even recognize.

There are no failures in Soul—there are only dots on the journey to owning our fullest potential.

SPIRAL LEARNING

When you work and live with your Soul Fire, you begin to see that learning is not a linear, A-to-Z process. There is not always a clear cause-and-effect relationship between success and challenges. The Soul-full life develops through spiral learning; that is, it encourages you to expand—come back to center—and expand again. Spiral learning emphasizes movement that allows you to stay young, vibrant, and aware. Each time you come around the circle—and there are multiple circles contained in multiple spirals—you have evolved. Like climbing a spiral staircase, you move upward—you are elevated and can take a glance down and see your progress.

I have learned and placed dots through music, through several iterations of my consulting and coaching business, and through marriage and parenthood. Looking back on the way these dots have connected reminds me of the magic and synchronicity that is always at work—but not quite visible when we are living through each moment. It reminds me to trust in that mystery.

When we honor our Soul Fire, we recognize our gift: *Our gift and the recognition of it is a contribution—it* *is **the** contribution*; our contribution is part of the whole that allows us to bring about more inner and outer peace—for ourselves, and for others. Shinichi Suzuki, the great violinist, educator, philosopher, and humanitarian, believed music was the best way to develop a character. He believed children who learned to play music would develop strong value systems, and this could ultimately make a contribution to world peace.

A friend to Albert Einstein and a man who believed in honoring a "life force," Suzuki died in his sleep at age ninety-nine. And though he may not have realized his ultimate dream and purpose—world peace—he did transform the character and values of millions of children and their parents across the globe. He also transformed the way music was taught globally. That three-year-old child with a tiny violin on her shoulder, or that five-year-old boy playing guitar, is Shinichi Suzuki at work, in terms of Soul.

FIRE IS NOT STATIC

Soul Fire produces harmony, but it is also somewhat restless and sometimes relentless—it checks in and asks: "Are you creating the life you want, the one that will allow you to depart the world when it's time, saying, 'Wow'?"

I believe Soul wants you to do what you were brought to Earth to do—carry gold. Moving beyond success as you now know it is possible because Soul is not limited by time and space or measurable results. It views life as an ever-unfolding story, and is ready for you to tend to it and keep its fire stoked.

CHAPTER 5

SOUL CARE:
WEAVING IT ALL TOGETHER WITH THE ELEVEN GOLDEN THREADS

It's probably clear that the conversation we've been engaging in throughout these pages is not simply about Soul dreaming, but about *Soul work*. Of course, I encourage setting time aside to dream, but in my many years of coaching and consulting, I have seen that dreaming only gets the Soul so far.

Even dreaming combined with strategizing only brings about so much success. If you want to live purposefully, energized, and fulfilled, you have to do some Soul searching. Once you've answered your Soul Call and have engaged your Soul Fire, you have to continue to tend to Soul.

Remember that Soul Call isn't a "one-time event": You'll hear it throughout your life. And Soul Fire is a fire—it will go out if you don't pay close attention, remain open to the mystery, and stay conscious of the synchronicities.

Soul Care is the conscious and intentional practice that supports soulful living. Soul Care practices can be:

- Grounding—they support the balance of the body and mind with the soul's inner rhythm. They support the inner growth journey.
- Nurturing—they assist in consciously creating and cultivating a healthy environment for both inner and outer growth.
- Healing—when excessive demands or stress are causing harm or stagnation, they can be transformative or rebalancing.

You will *need more energy* to do the work of managing your energy, so where and how will you get it?

We can take vacation or go on sabbatical, we can attend retreats and workshops—we can and we *do* carve out time for Soul Care. But a few weeks a year is not enough if we are serious about honoring Soul Call and Soul Fire.

Fueled by my own experiences as a daughter, wife, mother, professional coach, speaker, friend, mentor, and mentee, I have asked a lot of questions, and have listened closely to a myriad of answers. Since my earliest days at school, I have been engaging in the process of spiral learning. Moving along this spiral, trusting my experiences, my muses, and my mentors, I have picked up many tools.

I refer to these tools as the Golden Threads of Soul Care. There are probably *many thousands* of Golden Threads in the universe, and infinite variations of each one of those, but the eleven I present to you in this book are those that I use and that come up most frequently in my coaching and facilitating, as well as in everyday soulful encounters with others.

It is not your job to utilize or master all of them simultaneously, but to pull from any that serve you when you need grounding, nurturing, or healing. Utilize them to support your body, mind, and soul.

You have begun the alchemist's work of melding the gold within and the gold without. I'd like to offer the Eleven Golden Threads of Soul Care to help further support that bond.

THE ELEVEN GOLDEN THREADS

1. BREATHING

Breathwork is used in yogic practice, childbirth, the martial arts, and athletics of all kinds. It is also incorporated into many health therapies.

World-renowned health guru Dr. Andrew Weil, MD, refers to breathing as "a bridge between the body and mind and soul." In his book *Eight Weeks to Optimum Health,* he notes that if someone were to embrace only one of the numerous heath strategies he promotes in the book, it would be breathing.

I notice that many people do not take deep diaphragm breaths. In my coaching, I often tell clients to consciously work on their deep diaphragm breathing. To know what this feels like, lean over in a chair. Wrap your arms around your thighs and take a deep breath. Feel how deep it is. Now try to breathe that deeply while sitting upright. Try to practice deeper breathing throughout the day.

Breathing techniques abound and many have existed since ancient times. One I like to practice is the four-seven-eight breathing technique, which entails breathing in deeply from the diaphragm for four seconds, holding the breath for seven seconds, and releasing the breath for eight seconds. Practicing this routine twice daily for four breath cycles is centering and grounding, and it helps to manage stress and balance the body and mind.

I encourage you to consciously focus on your breathing and to find some kind of activity like meditation, yoga, or walking that incorporates deep, relaxed, and mindful breathing.

2. NO STATE OF BEING IS PERMANENT

Years ago a friend said to me in passing, "No state of being is permanent." Something deep inside me said, "Take notice," and I have lived by this friend's words ever since.

It is an innate human desire to want to live a permanent state of happiness and bliss, and many of us are fortunate to get glimpses of this state of being—where everything aligns and our Soul Call and Soul Fire are working together. However, nothing is permanent.

Owning our attitude toward our circumstances—positive or negative—is a fundamental freedom and is an important step in expanding our experience of happiness. However, understanding that no state of being is permanent, good or bad, has helped me—as it has helped many—live more in the moment.

When things are really good, I pause and am filled with gratitude for the abundance of goodness. When things are difficult, I look as quickly as possible for what the lesson is and remember this state of being is not permanent.

Is there a situation in your life right now that you are hanging on to, maybe one that is external that you don't have any direct control over, but that is causing you angst? Perhaps the thought that no state of being is permanent will allow you to let it go, and direct your energy toward positive soulful situations that you *can* impact.

3. FOLLOWING THE RULE OF THREES

Patterns emerge in our lives. Patterns of three reveal an ancient wisdom—land, sea, air; body, mind, spirit; Soul Call, Soul Fire, Soul Care—to name a few.

Especially when we are going through a learning experience that is challenging, it is important to set our need for "immediacy" aside, and to think before we act, react, or let the experience take us off center. Utilizing the Rule of Threes helps.

Depending on the intensity of the challenge or change, vow to give it three deep breaths, three hours, three days, or three weeks—maybe even three months—before reacting. Keep this pattern at the front of your mind and ask, "How do I respond to this challenge in a way that helps me forward Soul Call, Soul Fire, and Soul Care?"

Giving an issue time provides space for perspective, and since no state of being is permanent, then things can and often will change or transform quicker than we think. When an unexpected obstacle appears, when a situation seems impossibly complex, or when your thinking is muddled, breathe and "give it three." Consider the time you are taking in context, and keep in mind the intention behind the time, asking yourself:

"Am I grounded and centered? Am I jumping to conclusions? Am I giving this the time it needs?"

4. FOCUSING ON THE FIGURE EIGHT

Being more present is more challenging than ever. In my coaching, clients often complain about the distraction of email, social media, and the constant barrage of information that makes it difficult to center.

I like to use a horizontal figure eight—or the infinity symbol—to initiate conversation about living more grounded in the moment. I suggest pausing from time to time and imagining that the present moment is represented by where the two loops of the figure eight intersect. When my clients are lacking energy or feeling down, I encourage them to loop backward and identify their past accomplishments. They can then bring this positive energy of success into the present moment.

Alternatively, tremendous energy is available for the present moment when we envision our bigger, more Soul-full future. Taking time to imagining the loop forward, which consists of a compelling vision of the future, can be equally powerful when brought to the present moment.

Of course, we don't live in the past or the future, but we can harness the energy of our past successes and future vision to live more fully and enlivened right now.

5. BEING AWARE OF BEAUTY

I've tried to tread lightly with clichés in this book, but I'm thankful for the truth behind the cliché, "Beauty is in the eye of the beholder." Because this statement is true, the possibilities are endless for each of us to find our own sources of beauty. We have that favorite song, or landscape, or book. We also have all the new songs, places, and stories to discover.

Beauty is eternal and renewing. The fully fledged rose withers, but there is beauty in that cycle too.

Some say beauty is the antidote to fear. Why not test this theory out? Next time fear is hounding you, seek out beauty, with intention.

Beauty is everywhere, but if you can't find a single source of beauty where you are at one particular moment in your day, simply close your eyes and visualize a place, a person, or an object that is beautiful to you. Reflecting on beauty is free and can be grounding in the wink of an eye.

Caring for your Soul—centering yourself for the day ahead—can be as simple as taking the time to watch the sunrise before you begin your work or being more mindful of the nature around you. One small jasmine flower blooming on the windowsill above your kitchen sink can be your day's dose of beauty.

Remember too to honor and celebrate the beauty that is uniquely you.

6. MANAGING YOUR ENERGY

As you begin to develop Soul Sense, you'll become increasingly aware of energy—not only your energy, but also the energy that surrounds you. You will desire to answer more questions and make choices based from this increased state of consciousness. For example, what kind of food are you using to fuel your body? Are you aware of your food's quality and nutritional value?

Books on healthful eating abound, and this is just a brief reminder to say: Pay attention to the energy you ingest. Since releasing the weight I carried when I was younger, I've been an eternal student of which foods fuel my body and mind—and which don't.

What about the energy of the people around you? Are these people positive, future-oriented, learning, soulful, and desiring to make a contribution, or are they glass-half-empty, complaining, victims of circumstances? Do your friends support your Soul Call and Soul Fire? Do you support theirs?

In addition to your food intake and your social network, your awareness will increase toward the types of activities you engage in. Which activities give you energy and which sap it? Making changes to align yourself with activities that fuel your Soul Fire is an important part of Soul Care.

As you move along on this Soul-full quest, you will begin to understand how to master control. That is, you'll begin to see which situations you can control, and which you can't. As time progresses, you'll learn to let go of the latter quicker, and in doing so, you'll have more energy.

As you begin to focus with more intention on what you *can* impact, the space and time you have for taking in and generating more positive energy expands. This in turn generates more room for your Soul Call and Soul Fire.

7. CARING ABOUT YOUR SURROUNDINGS

Your home is your sanctuary. Caring about and becoming more conscious of your surroundings is important to Soul Care. Clean your space; make it move with music or the flame of a candle; fill it with the scent of flowers, incense, or essential oils; add sound to it with wind chimes. Put things in order in your space, in a way that impacts you positively.

Years ago I had a vision for a room in my home that would be a sanctuary, a place for reflection. We call it our "prayer room," and it has served its purpose brilliantly. It's a place to go when we desire to be more centered. Additionally, every important family discussion happens in that room, as all are asked to enter with their best self. I strongly recommended finding a room or a corner of a room to devote to Soul Care.

My daughter carried this Golden Thread forward when she went to university, and lived for two years in a tiny apartment. There, she became masterful at consciously creating a sanctuary in a small space. She set up a corner with pillows, devoted to meditation and reflection. A single shelf held her sacred items and pictures of people and places she loved. She periodically moved furniture around to keep the energy moving. It was her retreat amid the stresses of university life.

Simple things and small changes can make a big difference! Manage all of your *ecology*. The positive energy of your environment is the soil that nurtures your growth.

8. THE POWER OF REPURPOSING

I offer this Golden Thread when I see that someone has lost sight of their purpose as it relates to Soul Call. This issue manifests as frustration, or the feeling of "I'm just going through the motions."

When someone tells me, "The current activities I'm doing aren't enabling me to move forward with my Soul Call or vision. I have to learn yet another software program [or whatever the activity may be] and I don't see how this fits in with the bigger, grander picture," I remind them to pause.

Recognize that even with awareness, change can take time. Even with awareness, you cannot connect the dots now, or just yet. The activities you are doing right now may very well lead you to a place you cannot see yet.

Changing your point of view, even toward the daily activities that can sometimes feel mundane, can help. Repurpose these activities in the context of the bigger picture consciously, and you can breathe new energy into them.

9. CHECKING YOUR ASSUMPTIONS

On the well-known *Humans of New York* website, photographer Brandon Stanton captures two eye doctors sitting on a park bench. He asks them, "What's something about the eye that most people don't realize?"

One of the doctors answers, "The eye doesn't see. The brain sees. The eye just transmits. So what we see isn't only determined by what comes through the eyes. What we see is affected by our memories, our feelings, and by what we've seen before."

What an excellent reminder on the importance of checking our assumptions. We may come across a person or a situation and make judgments without realizing we are doing so. If I greet a colleague in the morning and receive nothing but a cursory grunt back, I could easily spiral down the "What an unpleasant person. What is wrong with him?" and then straight into "What'd I do wrong?"

I could start right down the path of worry for the next hour—or all day.

What a senseless drain of energy. Most likely, other people's reactions to you are merely reflections of factors beyond your control that have nothing to do with you. Maybe this colleague suffered insomnia the night before because of an important presentation coming up—and now he's worried he won't come across as alert and brilliant as usual.

We make stuff up all the time, and spend so much energy doing so, that we end up believing in the make-believe. We then spend more energy worrying about what we've made up: "Oh, it must be something I did!"

Don't assume the worst. We never know what another human being is going through or showing up with when we happen to cross paths with them. Check in with your own assumptions first and, if appropriate and possible, check in with the person to verify the truth of your assumption. When we pause instead of making assumptions on a more regular basis, we can gain back more purposeful energy.

10. FINDING YOUR MUSE

Being an adult is serious business, which is why it is so important to find your creative outlet. In the traditional Greek sense, the Muses were linked to the arts and the Garden of the Muses was a place to find or rekindle your inspiration. But your Muse can exist anywhere: it could exist in a fly fishing tackle box, in a community garden, or in the dynamic of a boardroom.

Whatever brings you the kind of bliss that takes your mind off of everything else—whatever lands you in a state of reverie—is your Muse. So play with it!

Muse-inspired play keeps us balanced. Multiple studies have come out on the value of play, even in professional contexts. Opportunities to play are everywhere. Inspired people have more fun at work and at home, and they inspire others around them.

Play as a catalyst for creativity and bonding makes Soul Sense *and* scientific sense. When we sing, or dance, or otherwise engage our Muse, we breathe deeply and our brain chemistry changes. Laughter releases endorphins, which can relieve pain. Singing together releases oxytocin, a hormone that enhances feelings of trust.

George Bernard Shaw said, "We don't stop playing because we grow old; we grow old because we stop playing."

Try to see your work and your learning as play—not as separate entities—and you won't grow old. Two of the greatest music educators that have inspired me—Shinichi Suzuki and Marcel Moyse—both lived into their nineties!

11. LIFE INFORMS VISION

Sometimes along the success track, we get stuck. Success has been defined as A, B, C, and we become fixated on certain goals. But remember, learning is spiral. Fixation is unhealthy. Fire is not static, the Soul seeks movement, and the ability to shift our point of view is crucial.

At certain moments, we realize that for whatever reason, we have not been listening closely enough to life's messages. In times of volatility, the rush of that volatility itself can get in the way of our paying attention. However, it is in the most tumultuous times that we need to be most attentive, agile, and flexible.

Let the circumstances of life feed into your vision, listen carefully, and adjust your vision to be congruent with the signs your soul is giving you.

Not long ago, I traveled to Greece with a tour group. Greece had been a dream destination of mine since childhood—I was connected to the place, but I didn't know how.

Several days into our trip, before we were scheduled to visit the Oracle of Delphi, our wise and attentive guide, Phil Cousineau, told us to prepare a question for the Oracle. In another time and place, I might have considered the visit just another amazing step on the itinerary, but instead, I made a conscious decision to figure out what question I really wanted to ask. I took it seriously.

And so, I went to the Oracle of Delphi and asked, "What are the keys to inspiration so I can go back and serve with them? How can I become an instrument to help people connect to their hope, through inspiration?"

I let life inform vision, and this book is a result of what happened when I asked a deep soulful question—and surrendered.

CLOSING THOUGHTS

A CALL TO CHOOSE

This book is about choice and the belief that we do have the capacity, wisdom, and power to respond to whatever the universe tosses our way—be it economic instability or prosperity, professional challenges or triumphs, personal hardships or successes. I believe that in difficult situations, and in the best of times, we can choose to develop greater Soul Sense and live more soulfully.

With the technological advances that make our lives simpler also come advances that force us to adapt more rapidly than ever. Not that we can't do it—we are adapting—but change and volatility undeniably cause instability. None of us is immune from veering off-center from time to time.

There is a huge opportunity to expand our consciousness and take root in Soul so that we can ride this instability out with greater grounding and purpose.

We have the power to choose to expand our success formula to include soulful living and leadership in everyday life. I have made the choice, as have many others I meet and coach—to develop Soul Sense, to listen deeply for Soul Call, to let the spark of this Call ignite Soul Fire, and to mindfully practice Soul Care. Of course, we cannot know in advance what any of our choices will amount to down the road—the dots that form the patterns of our lives show up mostly in hindsight—but so long as the choices we make are informed through our willingness to listen, create, and take risks via Soul, we can trust in them.

When you consciously choose to make Soul part of your ongoing journey, you become more aware of synchronicities. You realize that life has a funny way of showing up for you, once you start listening.

The fact that you were drawn to this book is synchronicity and Soul Call in action. Suddenly, people telling you exactly what you have long needed to hear and hidden opportunities presenting themselves are a result of you having decided to interface more consciously and accountably with life.

You have enacted the Soul Sense Process™. Your Soul Call has been activated. Start journaling your Soul Sounding and Moments of Soul discoveries, making note of any and all synchronicities. As you do this on a regular basis, patterns, insights, or messages may eventually emerge that confirm this path you have chosen to take—or that give you the courage to make some long-needed changes. Become increasingly aware of what activities inspire and energize you. Focusing more time on these activities will stoke your Soul Fire and bring more *energeia* and vitality into your daily life.

Continuously and consciously turn to the Eleven Golden Threads and practice Soul Care. Discover and practice your own Golden Threads—adding to this list of eleven, anything that nurtures, grounds, and centers you. Give Soul space, time, and respect through some form of ritual—even for just five minutes at the start of each day.

I believe the benefits of conscious soulful living are abundant: You will experience more vitality, you will be more confident that you are on your path, and you will see more evidence of your contribution. Outside forces can spin all they want—you will be able to stay grounded.

Your spiral of learning never ends, and you understand that the most honorable choice you can make during your time on this great swirling planet is to carry and spread your light—your Soul Fire and all its gifts—into your corner of the world.

Each of us has a unique contribution to offer—we can always learn, achieve, and give more. When you think of people who have changed the world through art or technology or science, consider the reality that *you* can change the world too—even if that simply means you end the day saying, "Wow! Today, I did my best to bring forth my gift and share it—today I chose to respond with soul and make a positive impact."

Choice can contain hope. And hope always contains possibility. You can make the necessary changes to soulfully create and live the life you want. The Beatles sang, in "Blackbird": "All your life you were only waiting for this moment to arise. You were only waiting for this moment to be free, you were only waiting…"

I believe the moment to consciously develop Soul Sense is now. I invite you to choose it!

ACKNOWLEDGMENTS

No book is completed without the support of many individuals. I would first like to acknowledge my husband and business partner, Patrick James Duffy, for his continuous support throughout this project. His encouragement, input, and many conversations helped to form the nucleus of this book. Patrick, I am truly grateful for your contribution and love. Our experience together lives on each page of this book: I love you.

To the many clients of Big Futures Inc.—thank you for your willingness to learn, grow, and transform in realizing your bigger, more successful, and Soulful futures. Thank you for your courage and determination to go to the Moon and beyond within The Moon Project® program. *Soul Sense* would not be possible without the learning and support you have given us.

To Dan Sullivan and Babs Smith and the team and clients of The Strategic Coach Inc., thank you for your incredible partnership. As an Associate Coach I am truly blessed to be part of the learning and transformation of hundreds of Soulful entrepreneurs risking to create their unique value in the world.

To my dear friend and mentor Phil Cousineau— thank you for the learning, the encouragement, and the spiritual pilgrimage trip to Greece. You are indeed an example of Soul-full living and leadership in action.

To David Hancock, Tiffany Gibson and Jim Howard of Morgan James Publishing – with deep appreciation for believing in me and in Soul Sense. To the editing team Michael Levin and Christine Fadden – thank you for your professionalism and expertise.

With eternal gratitude to my parents Elizabeth Moore Arlen and George Arlen. The original idea for a book on Soul-full living and leadership came upon their passing.

To my wonderful family—for all of your support— and especially to my daughter and best friend Clara Ailene, for your amazing Soul Sense and Soulful leadership at such a young age, which brings me incredible hope for the future of our world.

ABOUT ADRIENNE DUFFY

Adrienne Arlen Duffy, co-founder and partner of Big Futures Inc., is an innovative leadership coach, speaker, and consultant whose influence, knowledge, and unique approach helps individuals, entrepreneurs, corporations, and non-profit organizations achieve greater results and more fulfilling success. Working internationally, Adrienne focuses on vision, strategy, and accountability—but to that powerful mix, she adds what she has found to be an essential ingredient: Soul Sense. Additionally, Adrienne leads workshops for hundreds of entrepreneurs quarterly via her long-term alliance as an Associate Coach with The Strategic Coach®.

Since the late 1990s when she created The Moon Project® with her business partner and husband, Patrick James Duffy, Adrienne has been listening to the stories of the many people she mentors and guides. She has found that leaders and individuals, more than ever before, are looking for a more soulful way to live and lead.

If you've enjoyed this book and would like to get in touch with me, contact:

Adrienne@mysoulsense.com
www.mysoulsense.com
www.bigfuturesinc.ca

SOUL SENSE:
TAKING ACTION

1. Soul Call: What situations can you commit your *best self* to today?

_____

_____

_____

_____

2. Soul Fire: What inspires you today?

_____

_____

_____

_____

3. Soul Care: What can you do to nurture your body, mind or Soul today?

_____

_____

_____

_____

Morgan James
Speakers Group

www.TheMorganJamesSpeakersGroup.com

We connect Morgan James published authors with live and online events and audiences whom will benefit from their expertise.

Morgan James makes all of our titles available through the Library for All Charity Organization.

www.LibraryForAll.org

Printed in the USA
CPSIA information can be obtained
at www.ICGtesting.com
JSHW080004150824
68134JS00021B/2276